THE SAMSON SYNDROME

THE RISE, FALL, AND RESTORATION OF A GODLY MAN

PASTOR PHILLIP S. WILLIAMS, JR

ACKNOWLEDGEMENTS

I would like to take this opportunity to dedicate this book to some very important people in my life. First and foremost, to my Lord and Savior, for the gift He placed in me and the passion to share it.

To my family & friends, I appreciate all the years of love, encouragement, and unwavering support. Love you all.

To my spiritual Father, Pastor Rogerstein Gourdine and the Applied Word Church Family, you have watched me grow from a little boy into the man of God I am today. Thank you for always believing in my calling and giving me a great example of what a true man of God should be. Thank you for your uncompromising stance and being the Leader I needed to see.

Most importantly, to my three amazing children: Joshua, Jonathan, and Jessica. As great of an accomplishment this book is in my life, you three will always be my greatest accomplishments. I love each of you more than words can ever express and I am so grateful that God saw fit to allow me the honor of being your Dad. Thank you for being my daily inspiration. I pray that all your dreams in life come true. No matter what, always believe in yourselves, always believe that you belong, always believe that God has a plan for your lives. You can do anything, be anything, go anywhere…but always remember to take the Lord with you every step of the way.

TABLE OF CONTENTS

"I knew you before I formed you in your mother's womb. Before you were born I set you apart and appointed you as my prophet to the nations." Jer. 1:5 NIT

INTRODUCTION

Many years ago a commercial came out for a company that advertised a bracelet that was designed to aid in getting help to an elderly person during an emergency or a fall. In the commercial, the actress, who was an elderly lady, fell down a flight of stairs inside her home while alone. She immediately pressed the button on the medical bracelet and uttered those famous words; "Help, I've fallen, and I can't get up." Also, you may recall the childhood nursery rhyme of Humpy Dumpy, who had a great fall and all the king's horses and men, could not put him back together again.

What happens when a man falls so hard that he really can't get back up or a public failure hits his life so traumatically that nothing and no one can seemingly put him back together again? Men who cannot find any place to run for restoration in their lives and consequently become part of a society full of broken men who believe wholeheartedly that they will never recover from the mistakes and failures of their past. Men who have lost their way because they became intoxicated off the arrogance of themselves. The Bible says in Proverbs 24:16 "For a righteous man falls seven times, and rises again, but the wicked stumble in time of calamity." (NIV) The encouragement in the verse is in the rising again; however, the blessing is in both the fall and the rise. For there are valuable lessons tucked away in both a man's failure and his will to succeed again.

Every man has fallen susceptible to the Sampson Syndrome in life and many find their way through to total healing and deliverance; however, a lot of men get trapped and carry this *"illness"* with them their entire lives and never become the man that God ordained them to be. Somehow during the process, they forgot a valuable lesson: It's not how many times a man is knocked down, but how many times he decides to get back up again. It's time to get back up again.

This book is written to that man who has walked away from his passion, retreated into his cave of grief, loneliness, depression, and self-pity. That failure, although enormous in your eyes, is not bigger than the love and grace of the Lord Jesus Christ. God's grace is bigger than your disgrace. You may have fallen, and you feel you can't get up again, but help is on its way for you. Perhaps your life may be nothing but broken pieces of the man you desired to become but fell far short, but there is somebody that can put you back together again.

CHAPTER 1
I AM SAMSON

There is not a man that I know who would view being compared to Samson as a compliment outside of his masculine prowess. Most men would be openly offended by the comparison while others spend their entire lives trying to hide their character flaws by creating the façade of a different type of man. The truth of the matter remains that no matter how much we try to distance ourselves from Samson, there is so much of his struggle that resonates with men today. There are no new struggles in manhood. Samson was born with a destiny, a divine purpose by God to be used as a deliverer of the Israelites from the hand of the Philistines. Samson was given supernatural strength by God to overcome the numerous challenges he would face, as well as, to perform heroic and utterly amazing feats such as killing a lion, destroying a pagan temple, and even slaying an entire army with the jawbone of an ass.

From the outside, Samson was on top of the world. He was excelling at every challenge that he faced in his life. He had built a name and reputation for himself that was to be respected. Samson had two internal vulnerabilities: his secret to his strength and his overpowering lust for women. These vulnerabilities both ultimately proved to be significant in his demise and death. At this point, you may be asking yourself "How Am I Samson?" Well, most men are succeeding in the marketplace, in the boardroom, on the sports and practice fields, and on the biggest stages this world has to offer, but once the lights dim and the crowds go home and there is no one left to impress with their charm, good looks, degrees, or words….there only remains the man himself to be dealt with.

These men daily step off the stage of public success and succumb immediately back into their private lives of personal failure and struggle. There are great men and men that can become great, but with greatness comes controversy because greatness forces you to deal with the Samson inside of you. Samson is a part of the real you, the darkest part of you that you've locked so far down inside of yourself hoping that he never finds his way out. He represents the best and the worst in you. A blessing and a curse at the same time. He is the face of all your failures, disappointments, frustrations, addictions, phobias, fears, and struggles. He is in your dreams and for many; he is a nightmare that won't seem to go anywhere. You eat with him, bathe with him, lay down with him, and no matter how much you succeed he will not let you feel you're ever good enough.

Samson represents not only the ego of a man but also the arrogance of a man who refuses to bring himself under the headship of Christ because he doesn't understand that manhood and Christlikeness are equivalent to one another. True manhood is not something that is discovered or taught in the streets by broken men who never were taught themselves how to be men. They covered up their failures at being husbands, fathers, and leaders in their respective communities under the false banner of "Manhood". We have been passing down from generation to generation a false perception of what true manhood is supposed to entail. The sad reality is that a lot of our forefathers of previous generations were not man enough to deal with their demons and instead of passing on wisdom to the next generation, they passed on arrogance. This is one of the major factors as to why males today can still father children and walk away from the responsibility of raising them. While our women struggle trying to raise boys into men without any firsthand knowledge of the inner workings of what is needed.

This arrogance is as strong today as it was with Samson because he relied on his strengthens while ignoring his weaknesses. This arrogance is the underlying cause for extramarital affairs, divorces, absence of fathers, among other social ills within our society. Arrogance and pride are major symptoms of a man who is infected with the Samson Syndrome. And just like one can walk around infected by natural disease and never know, many men are walking around infected and do not know. Perhaps we do not know because we are taught as men to embrace our ego's and somehow this type of negative arrogance and pride has become an all-consuming ideology that is now embraced in a self-absorbed and shallow society who have foolishly placed their confidence in themselves instead of God.

Scripture seems to support the notion that warns us repeatedly against this type of pride and arrogance. Proverbs 16:18 speaks, "Pride goes before destruction, and haughtiness before a fall" (NIV). Many other scriptural references uphold the fact that pride is always at the center of any man's demise. Even in the medical arena, it is a proven fact that more African American males die due to treatable illnesses, including cancers, because they waited too long to seek medical treatment. I can attest to this growing up where black men were too prideful about going to the doctor's office concerning their well being. That pride prevented early detection, and many died horrible deaths of great suffering. It wasn't that they didn't have insurance, or access to proper healthcare, or transportation to get to these facilities for treatment. It was their pride that robbed them of a better quality of life, from walking down the aisle with their daughter on her wedding day, from celebrating their 50th wedding anniversary with the love of their lives, and from seeing their sons grow up and take over the companies they built from the ground up. Yes, these men died with incomplete and unfulfilled destinies and died frustrated because by the time they realized their real illness wasn't cancer, but their pride, it was too late.

A man's perception of himself becomes the building blocks on which he frames his identity and measures his manhood. Men have been raised with a warped, unhealthy perception of manhood as boys that they carry over into adulthood and end up going through their entire adult lives as little boys trapped in a man's body. They grew physically into men, but remained little boys mentally, emotionally, and spiritually. Therefore, the outward signs become evident because instead of looking for his equal, he instead looks for his next mother. The mistake that a lot of women make at this junction is that she will marry him as a boy believing she can raise him into the man of her dreams. She forgot to first let God make him out of a man before trying to make him out of a husband. There is a real identity crisis in our world today concerning the place of authority given to man by his Creator. In Genesis 1:26 "Then God said, "Let us make mankind in our image, in our likeness, so that they may rule over the fish in the sea and the birds in the sky, over the livestock and all the wild animals, and overall the creatures that move along the ground." We see here that there is a clear connection between identity and dominion and authority, but there is an order that cannot be ignored. God said that they may rule, implying authority, but this authority was not given until the identity was established. In other words, man will never operate in his God-given position until he first reconnects himself to the God-given identity he was given. Another way to put it is that when I know *Who* I am, it is at that moment that I can finally tap into the unlimited authority that was given unto me by God to carry out the assignment that validates my existence on the earth.

The reason that most men are in danger of never coming back to this powerful revelation is that they've been operating so long off who they have become that they have convinced themselves that "Who I have become" is "Who I am". How can anyone become something that they already believe they are? Perception again shows itself present at this junction because saying "I am Samson", that's who you tell yourself you are; however, that's not who you are, that's who you have become. Let's look at this a little deeper to get a better understanding, you have trust issues because you were the recipient of infidelity in a previous marriage or relationship. You meet someone new, who has never committed any type of discretion towards you, but you find yourself struggling to trust that person. The reason why you are struggling is that you are attempting to build trust based on the person you have become because of the past. Would you still be a person with trust issues if you were never cheated on? No. You would enter that relationship with the full force of confidence and trust because that's who you are. You are a loving and trusting individual; however, bad relationships, lies, broken hearts, torn souls have changed your perception of who you are and affected your ability to freely love and trust.

I have discovered when it comes to Trust, there are two kinds of people: Those who trust until given a valid reason not to trust and those who will not trust until given a valid reason to trust. Which one are you? Which one have you become? It depends on which identity you have chosen to let define who you are. I believe God wants all of us to get back to who He created us to be in this world. I cannot allow who I have become (Samson) to overshadow who I am (Christ) and cause me to lose my purpose and destiny in this life. What is the principal factor that keeps men from reclaiming their stolen identities? Fear. Fear is the enemy of Faith, the belief that you can reclaim your rightful position and place of authority. Fear of people finding out that I am not as together as I want everyone to believe I am. Fear that if I leave this place of comfort and safety I will be hurt all over again. We never realize that it takes far more energy to keep up a false image than it is to make a real change.

When we say "I am Samson" what are we really saying? We are saying that we identify with his struggles, his fears, his insecurities, his highs, and his lows. There is not one man that can objectively look into the life of Samson and not see himself somewhere in the process and realize that he is failing in that area because of the Samson Syndrome that is in him. To acknowledge Samson's existence in your character is the first pivotal step to true change, however, it cannot be the only step. To acknowledge and never change only perpetuates the current culture of arrogance and pride that has already caused a seismic shift in man's ability to operate in his God-given place of authority.

CHAPTER 2
MISDIAGNOSIS OF SIN
(DELILAH DILEMMA)

I work in healthcare administration and I deal primarily with coding that is assigned to let the insurance carrier of any particular patient know what procedures were performed. The procedures come after the patient has first been properly diagnosed. I would love to say that there is a 100% success rate in diagnosing a patient; however, because there are many signs and symptoms that are the same for many different illnesses there is always the risk of being misdiagnosed. A misdiagnosis is basically when you are told you have one thing, but it is, in fact, something else, or it is that, but also other underlying issues. This unfortunate happening can occur on a minor and a major level. There are numerous horror stories of misdiagnosed cases that have led to limbs removed unnecessarily, even in some cases causing suicide and premature death.

Cancers that were not caught early enough and took years away from a patient's life expectancy.

Just like we can misdiagnose issues within our natural bodies, we also can make the same mistakes in our spiritual lives as well. In the natural, there is a book, called ICD-10, which lists every possible known illness to mankind. It is from this book that diagnoses are assigned. In the spirit, there is also a book called, The Bible. The difference in the two books is that the Bible lists many signs and symptoms for the spiritual illnesses of mankind; however, they all lead back to one primary underlying cause: **SIN**. As mentioned earlier, Samson was a man of great physical strength; however, there was a spiritual illness that was misdiagnosed in his life: his lust for women, but primarily for one woman, in particular, Delilah. Who Delilah is isn't as important as what she represented in Samson's life. As strong as Samson was he could not will himself off of the intoxicating desire of Delilah. She became a soul tie to Samson. What is a soul tie? A soul tie is a link to the soul that accounts for the influences that two individuals have on one another. They can be godly or ungodly in their disposition. You cannot see them, but you can see their results. I know soul ties are not in the Bible, but they are throughout the Bible. We see it in the link between husband and wife with marriage and through friendships, as Jonathan and David.

Those are soul ties working at their absolute best, building faith, trust, security, and camaraderie. However, this was not what Samson was doing with Delilah at all. Delilah served as a means to an end for those who wanted to see Samson fall. She represented his greatest weaknesses; however, a misdiagnosis occurs whenever we pay more attention to who she was instead of what she represented. Surely every woman cannot be nor should be classified with Delilah; therefore, it would be unwise to simply restrict every man's downfall to a woman...that's a classic misdiagnosis. After all, that's what Adam used as

his excuse. He blamed the woman God gave him while overlooking the blatant sin of disobedience, the real diagnosis. It wasn't Eve that caused the downfall of Mankind because the mandate was not given to her. Mankind did not fall until after Adam ate of the tree. Like Delilah, Eve was used as a means to an end by the enemy to steal, kill, and destroy the plan of God for mankind. The truth of the matter is that Samson already had the weakness before he ever met Delilah. She became the catalyst that the enemy used to exploit that weakness inside of Samson.

Delilah is a physical name given to illustrate the spiritual principalities that seek to destroy the plan of God in the life of any man of God. Delilah can be something tangible, as well as, intangible working counterproductively in the lives of men daily. If it is tangible, it may be in his love of things: money, cars, clothes, drugs, and alcohol to name a few. If it is intangible, it can be found in arrogant attitudes, cockiness, pride, vanity, power, fame, control, and notoriety. These negative attributes are then negatively expressed in the behaviors of these men from physical and verbal abuse, thefts, murders, dominance through fear tactics, and other behaviors in the attempt to usurp authority over another person or situation. Just as Delilah was persistent to achieve her desired goal, so does this pattern of behavior in men who are under the auspices of their own Delilah. Their "Delilahs" are equally driven to achieve a desired goal of total shame and humiliation and degradation.

Delilah's profession would never allow her to be faithful to Samson. Perhaps her own experiences with men in her past prompted her to be such a willing participant in the demise of Samson. We do know that money/greed was present and certainly a motivating factor, but could it have been much deeper than that? Perhaps Delilah had seen this level of arrogance displayed before but never had the opportunity in her past meetings with other men to bring them down. Or maybe she saw it in her father and used Samson as an opportunity to get some vengeance on behalf of her mother, whom she could never understand the steadfast love towards a man who she saw treat her so badly? We will never fully know, but what we do know is that Samson made the same mistake that men are still making today---assuming that Delilah would always remain faithful.

The problem with Sin is that it too can never be faithful to a man. I heard a preacher say some years ago, "There are 3 things that I know about Sin: It will cost you more than you're willing to spend, It will take you further than you're willing to go, and it will keep you longer than you want to stay." Sin always has her own agenda. The Bible says in 1 John 2:16 (KJV) "For all that is in the world, the lust of the flesh, and the lust of the eyes, and the pride of life, is not of the Father, but is of the world." Therefore, knowing what we know about Sin and her intentions, we cannot place any trust or confidence in the flesh. Let's be clear, there is absolutely nothing wrong in having things, even nice and expensive things, it's when those things have you that they become a Delilah in your life. Satan's objective is to make you believe that he has nothing to do with the Delilah you are battling within your life. Delilah didn't actually destroy Samson; she was the door the enemy used to destroy Samson. The enemy uses each Delilah in your life to knock on the door of your heart and mind hoping you will open up to him. It's a persistent knocking that plays on your emotions, as well as, your ego in the attempt to gain access to the secret of your strength.

Samson put his confidence in two things: Delilah and his own strength and foolishly believed in both equally more than he did in the God that gave him the strength. This is the misdiagnosis of sin, which allows you to misplace your trust in the created things instead of the Creator. Men are falling every day, in all areas of life because they continue to foolishly abandon their biblical principles and instead place their confidence in themselves. Men, who were blessed with a greater capacity to do things on a higher plane than others but began to trust in their own credentials and ultimately never reached their full potential in life. Just as with the Law, a man who represents himself has a fool for his client, so does a man who places himself as his own leader has a fool as his follower.

As stated earlier, a misdiagnosis can be a small issue or a bigger issue depending on what the issue involves. Sin can never be viewed as a small issue because it deals directly with the heart of a man. As it stands, the #1 cause of death is heart disease, which accounts for 1 in every 4 deaths and affecting significantly more men than women. Sin is a spiritual heart disease that kills twice: naturally and spiritually. Sin is a disease that kills 100% of those infected; however, it is a treatable disease. John 3:1-7 says:

There was a man of the Pharisees, named Nicodemus, a ruler of the Jews: The same came to Jesus by night, and said unto him, Rabbi, we know that thou art a teacher come from God: for no man can do these miracles that thou doest, except God be with him. Jesus answered and said unto him, verily, verily, I say unto thee, except a man be born again, he cannot see the kingdom of God. Nicodemus saith unto him, how can a man be born when he is old? Can he enter the second time into his mother's womb, and be born? Jesus answered, verily, Verily, I say unto thee, except a man be born of the water and of the Spirit, he Cannot enter into the kingdom of God. That which is born of the flesh is flesh; and that which is born of the Spirit is spirit. Marvel not that I said unto thee, Ye must be born again.

When Sin has been properly diagnosed in our lives, the only treatment proven effective is that prescribed by Christ. He has given us the answer, "Ye must be born again". Jesus has to be seated on the throne of your heart to assure protection and security from all the Delilah's in your life. We must take our heads out of the lap of Delilah and place them on the bosom of Christ, this is the only place a man can find true rest. Jesus said, "Come unto me, all ye that labor and are heavy laden and I will give you rest." Matt.11:28 KJV.

Sin's assignment is to steal that rest in the lives of Godly men daily. When a man cannot find rest in his home it causes him to look for that rest in other places. Sin is the underlying cause for infidelity, but can we simply say that every man has the propensity to be unfaithful in committed relationships and marriages? I don't believe so. Although, I will be the first to say that there are plenty of exceptions to this rule. One key factor is that we never read anywhere in the story of Samson where he was ever intimate with Delilah, yet she was able to get his most intimate secrets out of him. How is this possible? One would think that because she was a prostitute, she used sex to gain access to what she wanted out of Samson. She could have used the obvious, but she would have never been able to penetrate deep enough because Samson's need wasn't a sexual one, it was a need to find a place of rest. Delilah provided Samson a place of rest where his normal dwellings did not.

Again, this is not being stated to give any man a license or excuse to be unfaithful or to ever go outside the boundaries of his marriage because certain needs aren't being met. I strongly recommend you go to God because your wife isn't the problem. You must seek direction from the Lord concerning how to reach your wife in a way that will allow her to positively respond to your frustrations. A man that is frustrated in his own life will always be frustrated with his own wife. Your frustration in your own life can easily cause you to shift blame away from Satan and place it incorrectly and unfairly on your spouse. That perception will cause you to quickly forget that she was given to you as a helpmeet to the vision that God gave to you. The enemy's job is to cause that perception so that you begin to see your wife as insufficient and inadequate to meet your needs. Maintaining the right perspective towards your wife especially in difficult and challenging moments within your marriage will greatly fortify your marriage and make it difficult for the enemy to infiltrate while God is recreating a Garden of Eden within your own house.

It is your wife's responsibility to create a place of rest within the boundaries of your own home. When that place of rest is missing in the home, a spirit of restlessness can easily creep in the back door, but this is where Godly character and spiritual integrity must take over in your life. When God made Eve for Adam, she contained everything that Adam would need outside of God. Whether you realize it or not, your wife contains everything that you need. God knew exactly what you needed, including every unfulfilled fantasy and exploration, however; sometimes that "other" side has to be coached or nurtured out of her. Again, it's not your wife that's the problem, that's a misdiagnosis; it's the SIN in your life that has yet to be dealt with. Now, with that said, it doesn't completely negate the woman either. She must guard her house and husband against the spirit of Delilah coming into her household by creating a place of rest (nag-free) for her husband.

There are too many households that allow the spirit of Delilah to roam freely and she will never leave the confines of your home until you develop a healthy hatred or righteous indignation for her presence. In other words, you have to truly hate sin to eradicate the spirit inside. Let me say it this way, I hate snakes. This means that I want absolutely nothing to do with them. I don't want to look at them, hold them, play with them....nothing. I don't want to watch any movies about them, and I don't even want to see a fake toy or stuffed animal that's a snake. I avoid the entire snake exhibition at a zoo or park. This "hatred" of mines allows me to maintain a boundary that keeps me from purposely pursuing or placing myself in any surrounding that is known to contain snakes. The chances of me being bitten by a snake are next to impossible because my hatred won't allow for the association. I cannot say that I hate snakes, but constantly go into the woods and other areas that are prone to have snakes. Your hatred must be the same way towards sin in your life. You have to develop a hatred for that sin where you want absolutely no parts of it. There must be a complete disassociation, a total disconnection, from everything and everyone that has ties to that sin. This also applies to Delilah and whatever she represents in your life that is of sin. You cannot remain friends with any Delilah in your life because it leaves you in a place of true vulnerability to be betrayed. Despite how she makes you feel in your flesh, Delilah is not your friend. Sin is not your friend.

Have you been misdiagnosed in your spiritual life? Have you been told by others in the faith community that it is something or someone else causing the negative issues in your life? If so, you have been misdiagnosed and if you continue to ignore the real cause it will ultimately kill you twice: spiritually and naturally. Nothing is more disheartening than someone dying from a treatable illness. Sin is a treatable illness. John 14:6 says, "Jesus saith unto him, I am the way, the truth, and the life: no man cometh unto the Father, but by me." He is the only true cure for the problem of sin.

CHAPTER 3

THE PROBLEM OF THE MISSING BUTTON

Several years ago I was pastoring a small church in South Carolina and I purchased myself a new suit. It was a nice 4 button suit with a matching vest. One particular Sunday I decided to wear it to church and I proceeded to put it on, and I went into the bathroom to check myself one last time before exiting the house. As I was in the mirror making minor adjustments to my tie, my attention quickly shifted to my suit jacket. There was one of the four buttons that was pretty loose. I was completely aware of it and had every intention of fixing it, but I did not have the time to devote to correcting it because I was running behind for service. I left home and arrived at the church and when I stepped out of my vehicle instantly the compliments started to flow from various parishioners and visitors alike. Everyone was in love with the suit. I had forgotten about that problem with the button. Needless to say, I decided to wear the suit again several weeks later. I went through the same ritual as I had previously done beforehand which included a trip to the bathroom mirror. Again, I was making my adjustments when that button problem caught my attention for the second time. It was still loose and needed to be addressed but just like the last time I was in a rush and did not have time to fix the button. I left the house and this time the button completely fell off the suit and I was unaware of it. I exited my vehicle with the expectation of receiving the same compliments that I had received before, but every person that I approached said only one thing to me about my suit: "Pastor, do you know that you're missing a button?" There were no compliments anymore because they were now overshadowed by the problem of the missing button.

I shared that story because God taught me a really powerful lesson concerning character. Each time that I was made aware of the problem with my suit button I was in a private place alone. There was no one else present to see the flaw in the suit. I was given more than one opportunity, in private, to correct the problem and no one would have ever known that the suit had a flaw. Instead, I made the conscious decision to ignore it, and not do the work to correct the flaw, and ultimately what was revealed to me in private was now revealed to others publicly. I want you to look at the suit as your character. You wear it and you want people to see it positively, however; there is a problem with some of the buttons on your suit. The Word of God is the mirror that reveals the flaws in the suit of a man's character. While you are standing in the mirror of the word, God has shown you privately some areas in your character that need to be addressed. When He revealed these character flaws to you nobody else was aware of the internal struggles in your life. The mistake that men keep making daily is the same one that I made when the weak button was shown to me, I ignored it. It wasn't important enough for me to address it. It didn't bother me enough to fix it. I didn't give it a priority in my life and underestimated how much damage a little button can cause in my life. God has shown you the flaws within your character more than one time to give you a chance to correct it, but you have ignored it.

The problem with my missing button didn't cause me to lose a position, I was still the Pastor of the church, but it did cause me to understand how not addressing an issue on a lower level can escalate into a much larger issue on a higher level. I have seen so many great men of God fall from powerful places in and outside of the church because they refused to deal with the buttons in their lives. A man's talents and charisma will allow him to get the promotion or elevation, but only his character will allow him to keep it. So many men pour all of themselves in the obtaining aspect of life: the promotion, the awards, and the accolades of life, but forget about the maintaining aspect of life which involves making sure that they have the quality of character necessary to remain at that higher level. When you continue to ignore the buttons, eventually they always fall off and it's always at the most inopportune times of your life. This is not the devil that waited until you were up for the promotion at work to bring up your problem with women. It was God allowing the button to finally fall off so that what is hidden can now be exposed because you cannot continue to believe that you can live any type of lifestyle and still have all of the blessings and favor of God working in your life.

I believe wholeheartedly that you know exactly what is wrong with your character. You already know the flaws within your character because God loves you too much not to show them to you privately. Samson knew what his button problem was too. He continued to ignore it and ultimately what was shown in private was now made public to everyone else. I am reminded of a story about a man who was the mayor of a small town in a rural community. He had been the Mayor for years and built a repetition of being dishonest, a womanizer, a drunk, and had even fathered a couple of children outside of his marriage. However, on paper, he was an excellent facilitator with strong business skills and had acquired many acquisitions of major businesses to invest resources in the community. One day, after a business meeting that netted the biggest merger in his political career, one of the councilmen approached him with the idea of running for Governor of the state.

He convinced him that the entire state should benefit from having a leader like him in office. Well, this Mayor became so intoxicated with the prestige and power that the office of Governor would give him that it only took a couple of weeks for him to publicly announce his candidacy and intent to run for Governor in the next election. He immediately began campaigning and raising money and support for his bid and for a time, things were going favorably for him. One day, while at his office he receives a call from his campaign manager, who advises him to turn on the television to the local news channel. He does so and what he hears almost gives him a heart attack. He is being indicted by a Grand jury for corruption and misappropriation of funds, he is shown on video coming out of local hotels with women that aren't his wife, and now his illegitimate children are coming forth to share how he has denied them and never gave them any financial or emotional support. Within a couple of days, that Mayor suspends his campaign for Governor, resigns from the office of Mayor, was served divorce papers from his wife, and was arrested on the corruption charges.

Does this story sound familiar to you? I shared this story to illustrate the effects of ignoring the buttons in your life. You cannot go to another level until you are willing to admit that you have a problem with your buttons. His zeal to go to another level without doing the work proved to be the biggest mistake of his life. This is not just hearing another story of the rise and fall of a man, but another opportunity to be reminded that this could have easily been your story. The difference is that God has not allowed your buttons to fall off…. yet. You are still covered in His grace, but grace has a limit before it runs out. You have known about your flaws for years, but you choose to keep ignoring them.

Are you prepared for the catastrophic losses that will come your way because you didn't deal with the buttons in your life? The losses will far outweigh the potential gains. You have way more at stake to lose than you have to gain pretending that the buttons aren't missing. There are so many men walking around with so many secret struggles and refuse to acknowledge them. Only when our character is perfected by God will the gains outweigh the losses. The Bible speaks about Job and how his character was perfected by God so much so that when the enemy finally was able to attack Job in the most intimate and personal areas of his life….he was able to stand because all the buttons in his life were in place. He was able to pass the test and as a result of that accomplishment, God blessed him twice as much as what he had lost. Job was never arrogant about his circumstances and he never ignored the gravity of his situation. God wants each of us as men to walk and excel in this level of integrity and character.

Again the lesson here is all about maintaining and not just obtaining the blessing. It is the will of God that you prosper and excel in this life, however; He also wants you to have the level of integrity needed to keep it. The Church has been embarrassed too many times by men who refused to work on their buttons. There will never be any perfect suits in this world, but whenever we remain humble towards our flaws we are given the grace to shield those imperfections in our character while we are allowing the Holy Spirit to work on them so that in due season we are prepared to walk righteously into the next level of blessings that God has for each one of us. We all have buttons that are hanging on by a thread and at any given moment could completely fall off and expose our weaknesses to those around us but if we are willing to abandon our confidence in our own abilities, God will not allow what was revealed to you privately to become publicly known.

It doesn't matter what Prophet comes to town; they will not be able to see it because God is still giving you a chance to fix it. King David is a perfect example of what happens when we choose to ignore the problem with the missing button. When David had an affair and tried to cover it up by having his mistress husband killed, David elected to not fix the issues privately and therefore grace had run out and God sent a prophet, Nathan, to expose the missing buttons in David's character to everyone. He was now a public disgrace, but David was still a man after God's own heart. David decided to no longer ignore the flaws of his character and he presented himself to God in such a way that he didn't lose everything in his life. David did some great things, but everyone seems to focus on his failures in life.

The buttons are there to remind us that there is always work to be done.

For many men, failure to see the missing buttons in their lives is equivalent to not being able to see the wind. We never see the wind, but we can always see its results and those results can be monumentally devastating and destructive. What are some of the areas in your life where the results of ignoring the missing buttons in your life can surface? One of the major places that it shows up is in your marriage life. Marriages are suffering because of men who keep ignoring the missing buttons in their marriage. The buttons of intimacy, communication, openness, finances, and trust are just a few of the numerous buttons that can fall off any marriage at any given time.

It is safe to say that you are not the same man you were 10 years ago; however, that change inside of you can cause you to fall off the same page as your spouse. It's nothing to be ashamed of if any of these buttons have fallen off your marriage, but you should be ashamed if they have fallen off and you are completely oblivious to it. After all, how can you address an issue that you aren't aware exist? Take this moment and pause and take an objective look at your marriage. Can you identify the missing buttons? Are you spending all your energy trying to cover up the fact that there are missing buttons? Are you spending more time trying to present a false image to everyone that your marriage is perfect and complete? What are you doing now to fix the problem with the missing buttons?

Another major place where the buttons have fallen off for men is in the area of Fatherhood. We have become too comfortable in our society with the absence of men in the lives of their children. It is a major disconnection that we have become completely numb towards. I believe that there is a direct relationship between what the enemy did to Samson and what he is doing today to the role of fathers in the family unit. There was something very significant that occurred to Samson after he was taken captive by the Philistines. The first thing they did was took his eyes out. They took his vision away from him. His ability to ever regain himself was forever altered because he no longer had vision.

The enemy completely understands vision and the need for it in this world and inside the home. The man, Adam, was given the vision and his wife was given to him to help carry out the assignment. The enemy's whole purpose in the garden was to steal the vision and when Adam ate of the forbidden tree, the vision was stolen and the ability to see like God was taken away. A man inside the home provides vision for the house. He is the designated Visionary of the house. Proverbs 29:18a reveals, "Where there is no vision, the people perish..." Therefore, if the man is the visionary of the home, then we can also say that where there is no vision, the family perishes.

To remove the vision in the home, you must remove the man inside the home. Satan has done a full-time job destroying the family unit by removing the man from the home, thus removing the vision from the home. Our society is perishing because of the severe erosion of the family unit. Young men and women will always struggle with their God-given destinies when they have grown up with either no father at all or a father who was physically present but never assumed his role as a visionary for the house. Either way the vision has been taken away from the home and results of that missing vision is still affecting lives and families this very day.

Allow the Holy Spirit to continue to perfect you into the man that God is calling for in these last days. He desires to use men that are okay that their suits aren't perfect but are not okay with ignoring the work that is needed to be able to keep and maintain the blessings of God in their lives. What are your buttons that need to be tightened up on the suit of your character? What are you secretly struggling with that nobody knows about but you? What is the real issue in your life that needs to change? Whatever those changes are in your life it must occur before the marriage, before you decide to run for public office, before you chase the promotion, before you open that business.

Don't allow your zeal for promotion to cause you to ignore important steps in the process and leave you completely open and uncovered. People can accept someone that has fallen, taken responsibility, and did the work to rehabilitate themselves. You don't have to be perfect or free from flaws to experience blessings and promotions, but you have to be free from pride and arrogance if you intend on keeping it. Commit to doing the work to fix the flaws in your character. If you have an anger problem, go to God, but also go to anger management. If you have a drinking problem, go to God, but also go to AA meetings.

In other words, build upon your character in a way that brings honor and glory unto the Lord. Fix the buttons today.

Chapter 4

The Rise: The Will of a Flawed Man to Succeed

What I am about to say to you may be a shock to some of you, but you are not perfect. Believe it or not, as great as you are in many areas of your life, there is yet a flawed man that exists on the inside. Perhaps you have yet to recognize where those flaws exactly lie or maybe you have already identified them but refuse to acknowledge their presence. Either way, there is this insatiable appetite within every man to succeed at something in life. It can be very tempting to overlook your flaws on the way to achieving a targeted goal.

The truth of the matter is that after sin entered the world we all became flawed.

The desire to succeed in life should never override the principles of God in your life. There is a predesigned blueprint that God has developed for each of us to follow in life that will guarantee us success and longevity in life. There is nothing wrong with a desire to own the best things life has to offer, but we must constantly evaluate our character on each level. Failure to do this will cause any man to believe that he can now move to a higher level without having to address certain flaws that exist on the current level of his life. The only difference between those of us who are walking around free and those who are currently incarcerated is they were caught for their mess and we were not.

I sometimes wonder when I see men who have seemingly risen to the forefront overnight. I would like to believe that every one of them is there because they have done the work in secret and are now experiencing the fruits of that labor. This would be naïve of me to believe because the nature of a man won't always allow him to do things God's way. If we were to look across the board at all sectors we would find men in powerful positions whose character cannot support the weight of their egos. Men who are at the pinnacle of success right now and have developed an untouchable arrogant attitude since they have arrived at their desired goal.

Samson was no exception to this same attitude because he started to believe that he was unbeatable, indestructible, and invincible.

You may recall a certain professional boxer named Mike Tyson. I remember him very well and growing up my grandfather, James, loved boxing, but he didn't like watching Tyson's fights. The reason was that they never lasted long at all. There were fights that by the time you got up to get a drink and came back, it was over. Tyson was the undefeated, undisputed heavyweight champion of the boxing world. He had seeming rose out of nowhere and took the boxing world by storm. Everything was going well in his professional life as it would seem. Then, February 11, 1990 comes and a relatively unknown boxer by name of James "Buster" Douglas steps in the ring with Tyson. Mike Tyson was 37-0 coming into the fight; he was favored to win 42-1 against Douglas but was defeated in the 10th round by KO.

It's amazing how you can be on top of the world one moment and then the world is now on top of you. Unfortunately, it didn't stop there as there were multiple other occurrences in his professional and personal life before and after that defeat. The point of this example is to highlight the need to focus on your flaws as you continue to rise in this world. This is especially important to our younger generation of males. They must understand ignoring the flaws in their lives will eventually catch up to them later in life when they are seeking to advance in life and the kingdom of God.

Your will to succeed cannot be so strong that you ignore the moral compass inside of you to the degree that absolutely nothing is off-limits. Too many men are driven for success, money, and power that they become heartless and ruthless beings who would sell their own souls to be in the spotlight of fame and fortune for 15 minutes. They will stop at nothing to get it and keep it. They have lied for it, stole for it, and even killed for it. Proverbs 14:12 says, "There is a way which seemeth right unto a man, but the end thereof are the ways of death." It's amazing what a flawed man will see as right in his own eyes. It is also amazing what a flawed man thinks he can get away with too.

It seemed right to Samson to trust in his own strength. It seemed right for him to trust that Delilah would never betray his trust. The temptation to take shortcuts on the road to success must be avoided at all costs. I say to this generation of young males who feel that selling drugs or other illicit activities are necessary to succeed in life you have gravely been misinformed. I know many young men don't see the relevance of going to work every day on a minimum wage job when they can make quadruple that amount on the streets.

I am not advocating to simply become another 9-5 employee that is making your superiors rich. I encourage fathers to teach your sons about entrepreneurship and becoming fiscally responsible with money and resources as early as possible. I encourage men to own their own businesses and other streams of income that will empower them to become lenders and not borrowers and not perpetuate the slavery mentality that many of their forefathers adopted. I applaud men that think outside the box and create opportunities to help other men rise and live out their God-given purposes on the earth.

The message here undoubtedly is to stress that success, longevity, and character are all developed in how a man chooses to rise. The RISE is everything. Too many men put too much energy into working hard to be nothing in life. Men that have risen to the highest levels of success and have maintained that level of success for decades; are men who understood how important it was to rise righteously. You can never fall disgracefully when you rise righteously. Taking time to build honest relationships and acquiring things legally may not always cause you to rise the fastest in life, but you must ask yourself a very important question at this point: Do you want to be big or do you want to be effective?

Things that seemingly swell suddenly are usually due to infection. There is no right way to do wrong. If you lay the foundation incorrectly than expect whatever is built to one day collapse. We have allowed the media to give us a false perception of how to rise to success. The music videos glamorize street life with fast cars, sexy women, easy money, enormous houses but they don't show you the other side. The cars and houses are rented and there is so much bloodshed in the streets because greed is the controlling factor. You don't get to see all the grieving mothers whose sons had promising lives now cut short because they chose the wrong way....a way the seemed right to them, but the end was death.

When Heaven seeks to promote, Hell is always paying attention. No wonder it didn't take long in the days of creation for the devil to show up in the garden. He saw Man on the rise, and he helped to create a flaw that was not present in Man before: **disobedience**. This flaw would forever plague men as they seek to advance the agenda of God in their lives and this world. However, we must not continue to use our flaws as an excuse not to be the men that God has created us to be. We cannot allow social-economic status, racial makeup, income levels, or geographical locations to keep us from becoming all that God has ordained for our lives. Find a way to rise righteously because how you get to the top has everything to do with your ability to remain there.

A man is not defined by what happens to him in life but how he chooses to respond to what has happened. You must become comfortable in knowing that you are not a perfect being, therefore, failures are going to come in your life. You must be able to effectively manage those failures and make them into opportunities for growth and development. Remember, it's only classified as a failure when you refuse to learn and grow from it.

Before you demand the best in the world, demand the best of yourself.

Chapter 5
Secret Sins: My enemy is my Inner Me

One thing that you must understand is that as men we have 3 lives that we live. The Public- this is the life that we portray to the general public, the one that our coworkers and/or subordinates know. The one that our community and neighbors see and admonish. The Private- this is the more intimate part of our lives that we reserve and show only to our families and close and personal friends. There is also another, The Secret- this is the side that we spend countless time and exert energy to hide and cover-up from everybody, even the spouse that lays in the bed next to him every night. For you to have secret sins, there has to be a secret life.

I have heard stories of women who spent years married to a man that was living a secret life she knew nothing about. A lot of men are so ashamed of their past that they go to great lengths to hide certain details about themselves. The unfortunate reality is that no matter how many years you spend with someone you will only know of them what they want you to know if they are determined to keep it hidden. Men who hide entire other families, criminal records, mental issues to name a few.

Do you realize that you are your own biggest enemy? I am sure that was a shocking truth for some of you to read. Samson was his biggest enemy as well. He would have never been in the situation he found himself in with the Philistines if he stayed away from Delilah. Now we can certainly be like Adam and put all the blame on Eve or we can choose to be real men and take ownership of where we are in life right now. For Samson, it was not that easy because there was a deeper level of sin that was hidden on the inside of him, a secret sin. Secret sins occur in the lives of men who have accepted Jesus Christ, confessed, and repented from their sins, but still struggle with certain types of sin.

These sins hinder many Christian men from moving forward in their spiritual walk with the Lord and it blocks the anointing and blessings of God in their lives. Secret sins existed before you gave your life to the Lord, or before you rededicated your life to Jesus, but even though you have repented in the past from them, they are still presently haunting you and working against you. The sins of the past that you haven't shared with anyone else about yourself. Things your wife may not even know you're still struggling with nor your Pastor or anyone.

More directly secret sins are those you commit and hide after you are saved, the sin you are secretly committing which you do not want people to see or know. Anything you do secretly which you do not want people to see, hear about, or know about that does not honor God in your life is a secret sin. It may be habits like masturbation, fornication, or other sexual immorality, including homosexuality while perpetuating the lifestyle of a heterosexual man. One of the biggest secret sins that men struggle with is that of pornography. Many Christian men, even in the pulpit, struggle with pornography.

It is one of the strongest secret sins out there against men of God.

Pornography creates a false perception of sex and has negative effects on any marriage. Most men justify watching pornography as innocent entertainment. Others say that it's the best alternative to physically cheating on their spouses. A casual interest in pornography can over time turn into a compulsive addiction. It also is a gateway sin that opens the door to the most disgusting and vile of all porn, which is child pornography. Men who have turned into child predators and pedophiles, and those who rape, torture, and kill women have some connection or association to pornography in their past. Pornography is exploiting the weaknesses of men and is a Delilah in the lives of many men.

Pornography also affects the women in his life, namely his wife and daughter(s). One man confessed that his addiction to pornography nearly destroyed his wife and daughter. Both of them suffered from eating disorders and had suicidal tendencies because of his rejection. Every afternoon as he returned home from work he feared finding his wife on the floor with her wrists slit, because of her feelings of inadequacy. Later, when in counseling his daughter explained her feelings of inferiority. She saw how her father rejected her mom, a beautiful woman, and feared never finding a man who would love her and tell her she was beautiful. This man caused great suffering to the two women he loved most because he rejected them to fulfill his lust for sex. Pornography is an elusive search for intimacy and a cop-out from building a meaningful relationship with a real person. Meeting the need for sexual arousal without addressing sexual intimacy inevitably leads to disappointment and frustration. Proverbs 28:13 says, "He who conceals his transgressions will not prosper, but he who confesses and forsakes them will find compassion."

Secret sins are barriers preventing true intimacy with God. God desires a relationship with you, but He also requires integrity. God loves you and desires to have an intimate relationship with you. Therefore, when I say "intimate" I am saying "In- to- me", God is in to me but I am creating a barrier when I am holding on to secret sins in my life. Choosing to live in secret sin keeps me bound in fear of man and separation from God. For many years, homosexuality was considered a secret sin, often referred to as "being in the closet". Therefore, many men who were ashamed of that lifestyle took on mainstream roles as heterosexual men that married and even had children but remained involved in homosexual activities thus giving their wives diseases that included HIV/AIDS.

Now, the government has ruled that same-sex marriage is legal throughout the Nation therefore there no longer remains the need to keep the lifestyle a secret. The reality yet remains that just because something is declared legally right, doesn't make it Biblically right. God did not create a man for the pleasure of another man. He created a woman for that purpose. However, let's be clear that fornication or adultery in heterosexual relationships is no less Biblically wrong or immoral. God loves all of us, but He hates the sin in our lives, especially the secret ones. Governmental legislation should never become the determining factor of your moral compass.

There are other lifestyles that we want to remain a secret from people like drinking, smoking, gambling, lying, anger, jealousy, etc. These types of flaws that we don't want anyone to know is a struggle in our character and daily lives. As long as you keep it secret; it has power over you. It will cause you to live in fear over what people will say or how they will respond. The question is: Do you care more about what people think of you here; who have no heaven or hell to place you in? The Bible says, "And fear not them which kill the body, but are not able to kill the soul: but rather fear him which can destroy both soul and body in hell." (Matt. 10:28 KJV)

Until you open up every secret sin in your life to someone you can trust and put the sin and Satan to open shame, you will always be in bondage to those sins. They very well may be a secret where you are right now in your life, but they may not remain a secret should you desire to go to a higher level in life. Paul said in Corinthians, "But we have renounced the hidden things of shame, not walking in craftiness nor handling the word of God deceitfully, but by the manifestation of the truth, commending ourselves to every man's conscience in the sight of God." 2 Cor. 4:2. From this passage, Paul did three things which every man with secret sins should also do: 1. He renounced the hidden things; those sinful things of the past and the flesh. 2. He manifested the truth to men; confessing to the necessary people about the sinful and shameful things of the past. 3. He manifested the truth to God; totally repenting and never going back to such sins of the past.

I already feel in my spirit some of you men allowing your pride to rise here. You're saying right now there is NO way that I am telling my wife I cheated on her in the past or currently. I am not telling my wife that I am addicted to porn or anything else I've done negatively, I'm taking it to the grave with me. I understand the feeling because there will be parts of your story that others will never be able to handle. Some people will never be able to get past your past. Everything about your story is not meant to be told anyway, but this is where confession works its best in our lives as flawed men. Again, if I uncover the secret sins, if I tell on myself first…it alleviates the sting and extortion that others can cause with the knowledge of my past in their possession. In other words, if I tell on myself first, then there is nothing new to tell.

There will be plenty of people who love you in your present but would gravely despise you if they knew ALL of your past. Even the greatest Apostle, Paul, battled this same agenda when he tried to operate in his God-given assignment because there were still those who remembered his past as Saul. Again, I am not suggesting that sharing all your past would be the wisest thing for you to do in your situation; however, you do need accountability and an outlet. I certainly understand that you cannot share your secret struggles with any and everyone because it can easily be exploited and mishandled by that particular individual.

Even Christ, Himself, understood this value point of being selective as men of God to whom we show our scars to. You may recall that while Christ was present on the earth, 12 disciples walked with him. However, after he was crucified and before his ascension to heaven, he only showed his scars to 3 of them. Don't miss that...because you can walk with folks daily, and still not be able to trust them to the level of uncovering and showing the raw nakedness of who you were, who you are, and who you are becoming. You must surround yourself with Godly men that you can trust with your mess. We frequently talk about the pain in the pews and the suffering by the sheep, but we fail to focus on the great pain in the pulpit and those men who are suffering tremendously because they feel they don't have anyone they can be transparent with. The last unconfirmed report I heard several years ago detailed that pastors are quitting ministry at an alarming rate of 1500 a month. I don't know how accurate this number is but from personal experiences, it is certainly a believable number and a scary number. There were many times that I was done with "Church" folks, I was done with the "Saints", I was tired of the snickering, looks, the chatter and dealing with all the preachers who never once reached out to me.

This suggests to me that sheep have shepherds they can go to, but shepherds don't have other shepherds to go to. It is a shame that there is no concept of "one-anothering" amongst pastors. That a true pastor can fall, and every pastor abandons him and leaves him out there alone because they are more interested in protecting their own agenda and image. Where is the ministry of restoration and reconciliation? I've never seen so many men of God happy to see other true men of God fall in my life. Are you that jealous and envious of another man's anointing that you are secretly hoping for his fall so that you can capitalize on it? Are you that insecure about the plan of God in your life that you utilize another man's fall to scatter his flock? News flash…if that man is truly anointed by God he will not be down forever and what God has assigned to him to do will remain with him when he rises again. We read about men of God in the Bible who fell, we preach and teach their lives and how they were restored, but we treat our brothers in the Gospel with great condemnation and disdain.

I am not suggesting we condone sin, but we must learn to not be so quick to condemn either. The Bible has a lot to say about how a true man of God should live his life, but it also has a lot to say about when he falls too. I do believe there needs to be accountability and discipline in all of the instances, which is determined by the magnitude of the issues involved. I am talking about true men of God, which disqualifies a lot of them because wolves and false prophets are not under the same grace. We seem to live in a world where nothing has to be proven as facts anymore. Anyone can make an allegation about a man of God and before the sun sets he is tried, convicted, and sentenced in the court of public opinion. Therefore, knowing this is the new norm in our present-day culture, we must endeavor even more to walk as circumspectively as possible, but not to the point that we are diluting our anointing and not affecting change around us.

My best friend, who is a powerful, anointed, wonderful pastor of a thriving ministry in Warner Robbins, GA, has walked with me throughout many of my struggles and failures in my life. He never condoned my sins, but he never condemned me either. When I was wrong and couldn't see the error of my ways, he was there to enlighten me, encourage me, pray with me and love me because despite everything he knew I was anointed and he did not break my spirit while I was in my process. His friendship played a major role in my ability to finish writing this book. If you don't have a friend like this man, I pray earnestly that the Lord will place one in your life quickly. You need men of God who can still see your anointing through all of your mess.

You can no longer continue to be suffering in silence because of the secret sins in your life. God has called you for such a time as this and the enemy is using your struggles against you hoping that you will die without ever emptying out all that God has placed inside of you to do. You serve the God of the past, present, and future. Your struggles may be a secret to everyone else around you, but it's never been a secret to God.

The devil likes to condemn you all over again for what you have already been freed from in your life. In the judicial system, there is something known as "double jeopardy". This simply means that you cannot try to convict someone a second time if they have been found innocent the first time or if they were guilty and served their time. Now, make no mistake, we are all guilty of sin and all deserved death (eternal separation from God), but Jesus has paid that penalty on the Cross of Calvary for each of us. Therefore, we no longer have to walk around with the shame and guilt of our past sins. Confession leads to possession. "If we confess our sins, he is faithful and just and will forgive us our sins and purify us from all unrighteousness." 1 John 1:9.

CHAPTER 6

THE FALL: DECEPTION OF OUR OWN STRENGTH

In an earlier chapter, I talked about rising righteously in life and business because it determines your ability to maintain your status. I believe that there is a distinct difference between a failure and a fall. Failure is an intricate part of the process to rise. One must be willing to fail but not willing to accept failure as a concluding matter. Failure is another chance to perfect, recalculate, reconsider, revise, revisit, reassess, and come back to the table a better version of yourself. Failures can generate quick recoveries. Many of those failures are never even know by the general public. A fall is something different. Unlike failures that consistently happen regularly in a man's life, falls are the exact opposite.

They are rare in a man's life therefore whenever one occurs in his life the results are catastrophic and devastating. A fall is the sum of all unaddressed failures in your life. A fall is a failure unchecked. A fall is the result of a man unwilling to be held accountable to anyone or anything of substance. I believe a fall is God saying, "Let's tear down what you have built and start over again so I can be your foundation". A man that is now falling in public was already failing in private because of his unwillingness to deal with the failures. A fall requires momentum, it needs a buildup of smaller failures before it can express itself in your life. That is why when a man's fall becomes public; recovery the majority of the time is nonexistent because there are so many smaller failures that went unaddressed before it happens.

Recently in the news, we are now seeing so many powerful men in Hollywood fall because of their unchecked failures. Character flaws that went unchecked for years. Each story is strikingly the same...We, the public, hear about their huge falls first and it sounds so sudden to us. But as each accuser comes forward and tells their story...none of the stories are recent and some go back 40 years. Every story presented is a testimony to a failure that was not addressed by that man. These men could have stopped the behavior years ago, but they allowed their egos, statuses, power, and influence to overshadow their ability to rise righteously…and what we are now witnessing is monumental collapses among them all. They, unfortunately, share the same illusion as did Samson. Samson believed his own super strength would get him out of every situation and that falsehood caused him to continue to go unchecked. It was that exact cavalier attitude that led to his demise.

The failure of man led to the fall of man. David's failure to conquer his lust caused the fall of his kingship. Pharaoh's failure to heed God's warnings led to the fall of his kingdom. Adam's failure to obey God's directives caused the fall of man, and over 2000 years later we still have not been able to fully recover. The Bible says, "Pride goes before destruction, and a haughty spirit before a fall." Proverbs 16:18 (KJV). To make it plainer, Pride precedes a fall. In every situation where a man has fallen in life, it can be traced back to his pride. One of the reasons that this "syndrome" is so hard to diagnose and treat is because it lives under a strong deception.

Somehow, we as men believe our cunning tongue and charm and presence can supersede the need for God's presence in our lives. We have gotten so accustomed to lying our way out of situations or over-promising and under-delivering as a way of life that we begin to build trust and confidence in our flesh. Therefore, whenever we are backed into a corner, we rely on our own vices to deliver us from the situation at hand. It would be great if we all had the same level of integrity as the three Hebrew men that were cast into the fiery furnace. Although they were met with their greatest adversity, they did not fall. They stood tall and the Lord was glorified in their lives. This should be the desire of all men of God.

So why am I talking about men falling? Men fall every day and, in every way, imaginable, but have we become so immune to the falls that we no longer hold to any standard? We have gotten to the point in our churches where men are allowed to continue to operate and lead churches and ministries in their fallen state with absolutely no rebuke, no correction, no accountability….and most of all, no repentance. Therefore, before we will hold these men to a standard; we're quick to bail them out under the banner of "no one is perfect". We are not perfect, however, we set a dangerous precedent in the body of Christ when we have Leaders who feel they are above correction or accountability to the corporate body of Christ.

Pastors being caught having sex inside the church, being caught in extra-marital affairs, and then defiantly refusing to resign or temporary sit themselves down for a season because their pride won't allow for correction. When you are leading God's people, you don't get the luxury of "…only God can judge me"; the people have the right to judge the integrity of their leader and replace you with someone else better than you. We can make excuses for mistakes, but we cannot keep making excuses for outright sin. The church has become a cowardly joke in this present world. God is looking for men that will reclaim the standard loss in our world today.

I've only had one Pastor my entire life. I am grateful for my spiritual father when my failures were starting to show publicly, he made me accountable to him. I foolishly didn't listen to all the instructions he gave me, and I lost my first marriage among other things. I didn't have an excuse for my rebellion because I had a great spiritual father, but I did not fully embrace that rare commodity and the result was that I fell. They say live life with no regrets but let me tell you that there are many things I regret in my life. One of the main things I regret was my inability to have made my marriage and children my priority over my ministry. You may not be physically cheating on your spouse, but if you put ministry before your wife she will begin to resent your ministry as the "other" woman that took her husband away from her. Your children will feel the same way as well.

I was so busy doing the "Lord's work" that I forgot to do my job as a husband and a father. In my arrogance and pride, when she tried to confront me about having balance and fixing the failure, I attacked her as a hindrance to my ministry and not a help. If you are currently struggling in your church or ministry and can't understand why; the answer may be sleeping next to you every night. If you are mistreating your spouse, ignoring her needs, making her feel like a second-class person…your church won't grow. God won't allow you to prosper. Your ministry may swell but it won't grow. Swelling again is a sign of infection.

I am always amazed at Pastors that can counsel everyone else's marriage but can't manage their own. I know because I was one of those Pastors. I had the answers for everyone else's matters and none for my own. I suppose it was because my pride would not allow me to acknowledge that I was failing as a husband and father. My fall finally opened up my eyes, but the damage was done already. I am not intimidated by any preacher or his title because I am not a part of any secret clubs or demonic organizations that censor my abilities to speak the truth. If you mistreat your spouse, Man of God, God will not bless your ministry…….You will struggle mightily. You're wrong and out of order.

It's amazing the things you see once you have truly fallen. For me, it wasn't what I saw that shook me…it was all the things I didn't see about myself until it was too late. Even my relationship attempts left a trail of destruction like a tornado touching down in a residential neighborhood…I destroyed some really good women in my past because I was a broken man looking for someone outside of God to fix me. Perhaps that's why I can relate so well to Samson's life. He was looking for Delilah to give him what only God could give. How many good women's lives did Samson destroy because he could not leave Delilah alone? We as men make the cardinal mistake of mishandling great women who have the creative glory to pull the best out of us to be with women that pull the worst from us instead. Connecting with the wrong type of woman can be suicide to a man's destiny.

There is a specific reason why Samson's fall was fatal. The reason, in my opinion, is also one of the saddest things in the world to happen to a man. The final time that the Philistines came upon Samson, the Bible accounts that something was profoundly different in his life, the spirit of the Lord had departed from him. In other words, the anointing had left. Now, that is not even the saddest part of this story for me. The part that is the saddest was that Samson did not even know the anointing left him. If we look at this from a didactical perspective, this suggests that Samson had a seismic internal shift that transferred his faith, trust, confidence, and dependence from God to himself.

He forgot that his strength came from the Lord and at some point, begin to believe that it was by his own merit and abilities that produced his exceptional masculine prowess. Sound familiar at all to you? It's the storyline for a lot of men, great men, whose falls were even greater. Without the anointing, a man's fall will always be fatal. I know I am guilty of this at one time in my early years of ministry because I begin to allow the praises of men to invade the purpose of God, but I was blessed to have a Pastor who kept me on a leash and protected my anointing until it was mature enough to sustain itself in my life.

This conclusion should resonate with a lot of men. I have been in ministry over 25 years now, and I have seen so many men start out so humble when they were truly hungry for God, and God alone. They went to any venue to share their gift, did not matter the size of the crowd, didn't matter if they got paid or not, but then elevation came, and doors started to open for them, and venues and platforms got bigger. Now, everyone wants to be paid for everything…even the ushers want to be paid to hold the doors. These same once humble men are now Gospel divas, they deemed themselves "untouchable" and unwilling now to do anything to develop people or simply for the love of God. Every decision they make is driven by the crowd and check size. The truth of the matter, many of them aren't even anointed to do what they are doing. We live in a day now where talent is more desired than anointing.

Now, with that said I have been in ministry long enough to understand that it takes money to do effective ministry. I also understand that for some their ministry is their full-time vocation and therefore should be compensated and I get that you cannot do and give everything away for free because people will burn you out and people will try to exploit your anointing. Let's keep things in perspective because I feel the pushback already coming. I certainly know that we should present a healthy, wealthy thriving body to the world...I am not advocating for a broke, busted, and disgusted mentality to ascribe to. I am only addressing those who are fleecing the church as simply a moneymaking prostitute that they pimp their services out to.

There is a business side to the Church and for those who are truly anointed, pay them what is required. If you wanted a secular artist to sing and he said his fee is $10,000.00; you would pay it without question, however; an anointed Christian artist says $10,000.00; you want a discount. You don't mind paying full price for talent, but you want a discount for anointing? The anointing is free, but it cost.

Also, our anointings are at different levels in the body, for example, if you invited a certain pastor from TX to your ministry, and he asked for a $20k offering; he can require that because his anointing allows him to come with a $20k word. You cannot demand a $20k offering if you have a $200.00 anointing. I am saying that we need to get back to seeking first the Kingdom and His righteousness and allowing all the other things to be added (Matt. 6:33). It seems there is a flip and we are now seeking all the added things first and forgetting about the Kingdom and His righteousness; this cannot be our agenda.

We, the Church, cannot even delineate the difference between talent and anointing anymore. We invite "artists" and "preachers" to our churches to minister to our parishioners and they aren't even saved; they have no anointing whatsoever, but they are full of talent and charisma. The spirit of Delilah is out of control in our churches today…...the same spirit that Samson kept playing with that caused God to leave him; is the same spirit that the Church is playing with today that is going to cause God to leave her. Again, when that happens to the Church it won't even be the saddest part of the situation because just like Samson; the Spirit of the Lord will leave the Church and she won't even know it.

How sad will the day be for the Church when people get up on Sunday to flock to a house of worship where music and worship and singing and preaching is being offered up but God is no longer apart of the equation and nobody knows He is gone? It's already happening in some churches as we speak, but if there is no true repentance at the corporate body level, we will see it on an epic level. We can laugh all day at the old saints, they may have done a lot of things out of ignorance, but one thing is true-whatever they had it was real. You could easily discern the anointing and the Church had power.

Another reason I would like to offer as a suggestion to why men fall is that he is dealing with a frustrated timeline. What is a frustrated timeline? It is when an event occurs outside of the natural order of life that forces a man to deal with circumstances that he may be ill-prepared to face and consequently he falls. Let me explain more from this perspective, the natural timeline looks something like this: A male is born, from age 4-17 he is a student, age 18-22 he will complete college, age 23-30 he may marry, age 31-35 starts a family, age 35-60 work to retire, age 70+ he dies. Each of these stages along the timeline is important that they occur in a particular order so that he is mentally, emotionally, financially, and psychologically prepared for the next phase of his timeline. Let's say that instead, at age 15, he becomes a father, now his timeline is frustrated because he is forced to think and act in a situation that in a healthy timeline allowed him another 15 years to mature and prepare for. He is forced to learn manhood while still being an immature boy and that frustration in his timeline can generate a lot of "cause and effect" problems in his life.

He may not be able to finish school because he must get out and get a job. He won't get a quality job at 15 with no experience or refined skillset so he turns to "quick" hustling but ends up getting busted for illegal activities and is in jail for years. Now, his child is growing up with no father, his life is destroyed over decisions made. Men are frustrating their timelines daily by making poor decisions that carry lifelong implications. It is important to seek God for the blueprint of your particular timeline in this life so that you do not get ahead of yourself and be unable to handle things correctly. One poor decision can frustrate your timeline for years. Some men are in some complex and complicated situations as a result of their timelines being frustrated. There are no easy fixes to their dilemmas.

I will offer some key insight and that is to say this; the first thing you do when you find yourself in a hole is throw away the shovel. You have to stop digging the hole deeper than what it already is now. This means different things for different men of course. For some, you need to exercise more self-control---just because you can, doesn't mean you should. Having children is a blessing from God but having them with the inability or capability to provide and protect them is not. If you are struggling to take care of one baby; why have a second one? Why continue to frustrate your timeline? You might make cute babies, but there is nothing cute about leaving the sole responsibility to raise them on society because you're unavailable or unconcerned.

Also, you have to begin to make better decisions about life and it starts by discovering your purpose on this earth. Once you know why you are here; it makes it so much easier to begin to recalculate the direction of your life towards what you were born to do. This doesn't negate obstacles, roadblocks, and challenges along the way; it instead will inspire you not to quit until you see it come to fruition. Again, with the anointing, you can recover from a fall in life. The perfect deception of the enemy is to make you focus on trying to keep your status, reputation, etc. when you should be placing all your focus on not losing God. If you lose the position, don't lose God. If you lose the marriage, don't lose God. Your spouse may walk away… you can recover; friends may walk away… you can recover; family can walk away… you will recover, but if God walks away… you will never recover. Fight to keep the anointing on your life. It is the only thing that can produce recovery and restoration after a fall in your life.

Chapter 7
The Restoration: Picking up the Broken Pieces

I want to begin this chapter of healing by making a very candid and fundamental observation and lesson that I learned from Adam's story. In the book of Genesis, it outlines the encounter that Adam and Eve had with God after eating the fruit, which was the gateway to disobedience and the real reason for the fall of mankind. However; what was particularly interesting was the fact that immediately after the sin, Adam knew that he was naked. He then went and found a way to cover up himself as he knew that he was going to have his daily interaction with God. God came down to the place where they met daily and Adam was not present; God called for him (not because He didn't know where he was, but to let him know that He knew he was out of place), and finally, Adam comes out of hiding and presents himself to God. He is now "covered" in leaves that they sewed together.

The Lord then begins to inquire as to why Adam was not in his place but notice what he says (3:10): "I was afraid because I was naked." Not, " because I sinned," but, "because I was naked." The problem for Adam wasn't his nakedness; it was the shame. The reason that men cannot find healing when God exposes the sin, which leads to the fall, is because most men are concerned with the shame of their situation and not the sin of their situation. In other words, a lot of men care more about how it will look to everyone than providing the transparency needed for God to bring healing and restoration back to their lives. The first step to restoration for a Godly man has to be Repentance. You have to come into agreement with God on His position concerning the sin in your life. Shame keeps men from repentance.

Nothing in your life will get better until you fervently yield the totality of your being back to God. There is another significant point to why Adam responded the way he did. He couldn't call what he had done sin initially because he had never sinned before. He spoke to what new reality his "sin" presented to him. He was always naked since the beginning but never knew he was until he disobeyed God and all he knew was that he is now in a reality that was completely new to him. Sin was new to him and so was the nakedness.

When you fall now, sin is not new anymore therefore we cannot use "I didn't know" as the justification in the attempt to find grace or mercy from the Lord. I do believe that there are a lot of men who don't understand that their nakedness is not their issue because they are diverting all their focus and energy on trying to cover up the shame of their situations. Now, I am not letting Adam off the hook by no means; hence, why I said earlier "initially" he did not know it was a sin because eventually he did know and it was evident in how fast he throws his wife under the bus to God.

The sin nature had now developed in Adam's spiritual DNA and that nature immediately tried to shun responsibility from Adam back to God. It was now God's fault that Adam had fallen. This brings me to another step in the healing process: *You cannot heal from what you will not own as yours.* As men, we cannot continue to go around arbitrary blaming everybody and everything as the reason for our fall. I will be the first to acknowledge that yes there are outside factors that contribute to any man's fall and some of those factors are totally out of the control of that man. My point goes specifically to men of God who are fully aware of their sin and their nakedness but allow their pride to keep them bound to the point that they continue to willfully inflict pain and trauma on the lives of others. Men who would rather cause pain than deal with their pain.

Broken men don't get healed by not taking ownership of their pain. Stop and think back over your life and ask yourself this question "How many lives have I destroyed because of my unwillingness to own my pain?" Rage is pain that is out of control. Men may be the strongest physically speaking but we are horrible with handling pain. Men can cheat on women, get caught, and expect that woman to give him another chance. However, if a woman cheats on a man that loves her…do you know how many second chances she will get? I'll wait….NONE! We cannot handle emotional pain at all, but we can certainly dish it out.

Samson was foolish to believe that Delilah could fix his pain. Be careful who you trust with your pain. Samson trusted Delilah with his pain and the result was that she caused him even more pain than he could have ever imagined. The lesson here is for the men who solely believe that the woman that they are with or the women that they have been with in their past is the common denominator for his pain. If you get a better woman, a different woman, all the pain in your life will cease. God gave women to be a helpmeet to men. I believe the best place for any woman to meet a man and help him is on the other side of his personal pain.

This allows a man to be forced to look at himself and do the work necessary to properly address the pain in his life and not use his woman as the scapegoat to shun responsibility and accountability. Too often women meet men at the point of their pain and interrupt the process God is taking those men through to be ready to properly handle having a woman in their lives. Again, she must first allow God to make a man out of him before she tries to make a husband out of him.

As a woman, you may not have known he has an anger problem, a bad temperament about himself, but God knew and because you didn't let God finish processing him, you married a still angry man. Instead of him being alone so that he can deal with his anger issues, he is taking them out on you daily and blaming you for the anger and abuse. Do you really think he hit you because the food wasn't hot enough that you served him? God does his best work when he has us by ourselves.

This doesn't mean that we as men will never be without our flaws, but some flaws need to be perfected and dealt with alone, privately, so that the pattern of pain dissipates from our lives. I don't have time to talk about generational curses and spirits here but do know that they too have a relevant place in this setting as well. There are reasons why he has such a propensity towards anger, rage, or abuse and it certainly did not come out of thin air. Therefore, we must always look at the spirit of any man to gain real insight into his pain. If you get to know his spirit, you will get to know his pain.

I have had the opportunity in life to sit in on AA meetings and also grief support group meetings, both of which I am a huge fan of because we as men, especially in minority populated areas, have this stigma of going to any counseling. As stated in an earlier chapter, black males have the lowest life expectancy rating of 65 years of life. Even, if we look at it purely from a health perspective, we are the last to go to the doctor for preventative care. When we finally decide to go and get checked out it is no longer preventative, but terminal. That can no longer be our mantra to fixing the broken pieces in our lives. It is God's will that we live well in mind, body, and soul. To achieve that level of euphoria in our lives some time you need help mapping it all out. This is why I am a staunch advocate for counseling and support groups that help to generate necessary dialogue and produce those confrontational moments that are pivotal for a man that is drowning in pain to get the right relief. This will never happen until that man relinquishes the shame of his situation.

That's the only viable reason why we don't go to the doctors, why we won't get help for our particular addictions and struggles...we are too ashamed. We look at it as admitting defeat or weakness in our lives. It's impossible to bend an old tree. We are told as men all our lives never to cry but if men aren't designed to cry than the Manufacturer made a serious design flaw in us all by giving us that ability to do so. God gave us the ability to cry, not as a woman, but in certain moments and situations to show our humanity. A man that cannot cry at all is a ticking time bomb waiting to explode. Crying is a form of release, a coping mechanism intrinsically placed inside us all to help deal with the many disappointments this life will bring to us.

I've seen men stand at the caskets of their parent, spouse, child, or relative, etc. and not shed one single tear. Consequently, anger and bitterness begin to set in, and in some cases that aggression is tragically acted out either through suicide or inflicting harm or pain on innocent people. Again, there is a huge difference between crying with a purpose and being a cry baby. Some men are way too emotional about everything and that is equally detrimental as a man that shows no emotions at all. This is simply a call to balance and utilizing the available tools to assist you in achieving that balance.

Those meetings are given in steps…6, 12, or 20 steps but each are critical steps for a man to take to deal with the pain and broken pieces of his life. The broken can be repaired. Every day people throw away valuable things because they deemed them broken, and unfixable, if that concept were accurate then we wouldn't have any thrift stores, etc. Stores whose entire inventory is taking broken things and remaking them into better things thus making their value in most cases higher than it was originally. I believe that is what God wants to do with your broken pieces. He wants to remake you into a better vessel than you ever were before. Every individual that has seriously gone through programs like AA has come out as a better version of themselves.

Another key element to help men to recover is understanding how much his environment plays in his success. In other words, you have to change the circle of people in your life. If you are having marital issues, what is the benefits of hanging around friends that are all divorced? If you have anger issues, why are you hanging around friends that are as angry as you are? You have to surround yourself with men that are doing now the things that you want to do, who are already the kind of man that you are working to become. Men that will hold you accountable and also challenge you to be a better version of yourself.

Eagles don't fly in packs...but buzzards do because they are all about dead things. He may be your boy since y'all were in diapers together, but how is his constant presence in your life helping you become a better man now?

I am all for helping my brothers and those who I struggled with, but I want to illustrate a biblical point through Abraham found in Genesis 12. Here in these verses, God speaks to Abraham, about Abraham. He says to him, paraphrasing, that He is going to bless him, make his name great, and just do tremendous things and all Abraham has to do is leave his current surroundings and journey where God wants him to go. Sounds easy enough, except in verse 4, and here lies the same mistake we are still making today. Abraham goes and takes Lot with him; wait, that whole conversation with God was to Abraham, for Abraham and his response was to take someone irrelevant with him on his journey. When God speaks to us, we cannot make people stars in a script that was not written with them in mind. Some people in your life should have been cut off years ago and they are hindering you from reaching your full potential. They are the ones that keep disappointing you, frustrating you, and impeding your progress because you keep trying to carry them into higher realms and dimensions that they are not qualified to be a part of.

Broken people can't fix other broken people. Perhaps God is trying to heal you first so that you can be placed in a position later to be an effective resource in that person's life. That's exactly what God did in the case of Joseph. He started out in a pit. He had to first be delivered out of his pit and placed in the palace to be in a position to pull his brothers and kinsmen out of the poverty that they all were in. If the spiritual connection was missed here than let me come down to more practical terms: Let's say that you and your best friends' lights are being turned off. The bill for each of you to keep service is 100.00 each. You have 100.00, but your best friend doesn't have any money. Therefore, you decide that you will give him half. So you proceed to pay 50.00 and he pays 50.00 on his bill….what's the problem? Now, both of you are sitting home in the dark. Would not it have made better sense that you pay to keep your lights on and allow your best friend to stay with you until the resources to pay his bill are available?

I am sure you get the concept at this point. Sometimes it requires a show of selfishness first before you can show a higher level of selflessness. One thing that took me years to learn in ministry was that it's okay to say "No" to people and other things and not feel guilty afterward. The process of being restored is multifaceted in its conception because by the time most men truly get to a place of real repentance there are multiple layers that they have to commit to working through. Repentance is the first step; not the only step.

Let's talk football for a moment to illustrate a point here. So, for a particular play to be successful, it hinges upon those involved being in place. The Quarterback's job is never to throw the ball where the Wide Receiver is, but to throw it where he is supposed to be. It is the job of the wide receiver to run his predesigned route in a manner that allows him to already be in the spot where the football will be delivered. If by chance the QB looks in that spot and no one is there; he is then forced to hold the ball longer than anticipated in the hopes that the WR will be there momentarily. This action now puts him at risk of potentially being sacked which can lead to a fumble, a loss of a down, a loss of yardage, etc. all because the WR was out of place.

God has placed each man's deliverance at a certain place in his life and it is up to each man to do the work necessary to get to the place where his true deliverance is. I never said it would be easy or there would not be any opposition. Remember, there is a whole other team on the field playing defense whose sole job is to keep that WR from reaching the spot where the football will be delivered. There will always be opposition to you reaching your destination, but you keep trusting the process and you learn to build consistency and a determination to rise righteously and good things, better things will begin to happen.

CHAPTER 8
THE CURE: FINDING THE STRENGTH TO COMPLETE YOUR DESTINY

Real life doesn't always have a fairy tale ending to it when we find ourselves outside the will of God. Although Samson's story did not end with "…happily ever after" there are so many valuable nuggets that we as men can and should take away from his life story. We have seen Samson go from heights unknown to depths uncharted in his life. Samson has been stripped of everything; his vision is gone, Delilah is gone, accolades and prestige are gone, strength is gone…even the spirit of the Lord is gone. Seemingly, the humiliation of his situation is enough for any man to simply give up and die.

But, even if Samson wanted to die, and I am sure it crossed his mind numerous times, he could not die because he still had not completed his destiny. Samson's ultimate purpose was to destroy the Philistines. Hebrew 11 talks about Samson and concludes by faith, he "gained strength in weakness." That is a very powerful statement made in the text. Samson did not come to faith until the end of his life and through the events that happened to him in his life. The final scene of his life shows him standing between two supporting columns of the Philistine temple in Gaza. He is shackled, his eyes are gone, and he is the weakest he has ever been in his entire life.

It took this humbling process, this uncovering and exposure by God to get Samson to this point of his life. A point that he missed or ignored his entire life. It was at this point in his life, standing between two pillars, completely exposed, humiliated, and vulnerable that he finally understood that everything that he had ever accomplished in his entire life was not by his own strength, but by the hand of God on his life. The Cure to finding healing from the Samson syndrome in a man's life is when he finally realizes that apart from God, he is nothing. Apart from God, he can do absolutely nothing. Any time you remove anything from the source that sustains it, it will surely die.

Samson had pushed the columns down destroying the temple, but he died along with the collapse. The good news is that you are still here and there yet remains the opportunity for you to recover from your fall. Again, a fall doesn't have to be fatal in your life, but to righteously rise again you must be willing to abandon the vices that put you in the position you are in right now. You must be willing to abandon your confidence in your flesh. This does not mean that one should not believe in themselves, but that belief must be founded upon the foundation that God is the only source that supplies that confidence in your life. A man who gravities to the same habits that led to his fall will continue to repeat that same cycle in his life. I mentioned in an early chapter about "double jeopardy" in our court system. That the judicial system says that once a man has paid his debt to society; he cannot be tried a second time. This is true in the court of law; however, it's not the same in the court of public opinion.

If you are expecting to draw strength and support from people on your way back from your fall, you're going to overwhelmingly disappointed. You can't cross a burned bridge again. I learned that there are some relationships that my actions have destroyed, and I can never make amends with those individuals again. Yes, I now completely understand how much my actions towards them have hurt them, but in their minds, they will never see me as a man that understands the errors of his ways. Some people will respond in the same way in your life.

We do serve a God of restoration, but the restoration may not look anything like you anticipated. Your wife may never come back to you again, your children may never speak to you again, your community may not support you again, you may never get that job back again, but you must learn to now draw your strength from God. He is the God of a second chance, or third, or fourth. You have to be okay with the noise from the public and embrace those who are willing to see beyond your faults and failures. One thing that God will never do is restore us to the very thing that killed us in the first place.

There will always be a degree of loss when you are in the process of rebuilding. You have to become okay with those losses and trust the process of God. If it's meant for some of those people to be in your life again, they will certainly come back in time. We exert so much time and energy trying to make people stay in our lives who have already decided to walk out permanently. You are making the same mistake again by believing that you need these people to rise righteously. The collateral damage you inflicted in their lives may be too much for them to recover or forgive. Forgiveness doesn't mean that it has to go back to the way it was before. They forgive you for the sole purpose of them being able to regain strength so that they can move on in their lives.

Your true destiny many times wasn't even tied to many of the people that you hurt or destroyed therefore it would be foolish of you to try to reconnect them back to yourself. You're trying to reconnect out of guilt, not out of purpose. They serve no purpose in helping to fulfill your destiny, but they became part of your story because you invited them into your life when you were out of place with God. God wants to give you the strength to accept the pruning process that you will need to go through. What's the pruning process? If you have a bush or hedge that is not growing to its full potential, more than likely, it needs to be pruned. Pruning is the process of cutting away the dead limbs or branches that's impeding the continued growth of a thing. In other words, God is cutting to grow, not to kill. God cuts us to grow our destinies, not to kill them.

He knows exactly what and who needs to be cut out of our lives to allow our destinies to truly manifest in our lives. We love the growing part but hate the cutting part. There are many times when someone has been properly diagnosed that the only way to fix the problem to perform surgery. Surgery involves precision cutting. If the surgeon missing the cut it can lead to death. We have properly been able to diagnose the spiritual illness of men, which is Sin. Therefore, it will require surgery. The Word of God has been called sharper than a two-edged sword; cutting out sin and cutting in righteousness. For any man to truly be free from the Samson Syndrome illness in his life, he must be willing to allow the Lord to operate on his heart, mind, and spirit.

I began this book talking about the dangers of being misdiagnosed and how treatable illnesses in our physical bodies are killing men unnecessarily. Well, once you have been properly diagnosed with your illness, you then place yourself in a position for a prognosis. That prognosis can be positive or negative depending on many factors. The most important factor is a positive prognosis is early detection. The earlier a disease is properly diagnosed, the more positive is the prognosis. Poor prognosis inadvertently leads to an autopsy. An autopsy is a postmortem examination to discover the cause of death. We have successfully identified the problem you have is the sin in your life, therefore, there is no longer a need for an autopsy to be performed unless you continue to ignore the sin and it eventually kills you....twice (spiritually and physically). Don't die before you allow God to empty out all of His purposes inside of you. You may be in a situation where you feel like you want to die, but God has not scheduled an autopsy on your destiny. Your destiny is not dead, it's on life support awaiting a transplant. Romans 12 admonishes us to "...be ye transformed by the renewing of our minds." You must take out the old mind and the old heart and allow the mind of Christ and the heart of God to be surgically implanted through the Holy Spirit.

This book is written to help encourage men to come out of their caves and to truly begin to deal with their pains. The strength comes when we stop pretending and covering up and begin to face our failures. Your failures have not aborted your destiny, it's diverted it. Every plane that takes off has a predetermined destination to arrive at, however, sometimes unexpected influences arise that cause the plane to have to be diverted to another location to land, but it will ultimately reach its destination. Your struggles have caused your destiny to be diverted, but God still has every intention of getting you to the place you belong.

I want to share a story with you that I have heard several times in my life concerning a little boy and a bird. The story says that there lived an old blind man in a village high in the mountains, and he was known throughout the land to be the wisest man known. One day, a little boy thought he would test this old man and see for himself. He proceeds to get a small bird and goes to where the old blind man was sitting. He says, "Old man, I have a bird in my hands, tell me, is this bird alive or his he dead?" The old man doesn't respond. The little boy asked 2 more times the same question to the old blind man. Finally, the old man sits up and he says to the little boy who believed that he just outsmarted the old man,

"Young man, if I say that the bird is dead, you will open your hands up and let it go, and if I say it is alive, you will squeeze your hands tighter and kill it, so the answer to your question is in your hands."

You may be asking yourself as you have read this book, will things get better for me again? Will I ever recover from my fall? Will I ever be able to love again, trust again, and believe again? Will it ever get better for me? I cannot answer those questions for you because the answer to them all is in your hands. What I do know is that there is life after death, healing after pain, forgiveness after failure, and peace after turmoil. You must begin to see life as a circle, and not a straight line. If you will commit yourself to do the work necessary than restoration can and will happen in your life.

You may presently find yourself between two pillars like Samson deciding whether or not to push and let everything collapse on top of you. That was Samson's destiny, not yours. I believe that God wants you to rise out of the abyss of your failures and turn your pain into power instead. Again, pain out of control is rage, but pain-controlled equals deliverance. Men need to be delivered more than ever right now. There is at least one man that needs to hear your story and God is not going to allow you to push the pillars of depression, humiliation, and shame on top of yourself and forever silence your story.

I understand every man that reads this book will probably not respond properly because of where he is in his process at the time of reading this book. I hope that you never become comfortable where you are right now. Your sons and daughters are depending on you to deal with your demons and not passed them on to them to fight and struggle with. The longer you remain silent, the stronger that spirit of pride and arrogance begins to resurface in your life.

If you are seeking promotion or advancement, whether it's inside or outside of the church, please make sure that you work on fixing the flaws in your character first. Become a man of integrity and not a man of deception. Powerful men are falling like flies in our society today for things that should have addressed in their characters years ago. I don't believe we have ever witnessed anything of this magnitude happening with men. I believe God is trying to get the attention of men to get back in their proper place as leaders, who lead with integrity and valor. Men, who provide for their children beyond just the financial necessities of life. Men, who honor their women and relationships. Men, who show Godly character in the marketplace. Can it be accomplished you ask? The answer is in our hands.